LETHAL THEATER

The Journal Charles B. Wheeler Poetry Prize

LETHAL THEATER

SUSANNAH NEVISON

MAD CREEK BOOKS, AN IMPRINT OF
THE OHIO STATE UNIVERSITY PRESS | COLUMBUS

Library of Congress Cataloging-in-Publication Data
Names: Nevison, Susannah, 1984– author.
Title: Lethal theater / Susannah Nevison.
Description: Columbus : Mad Creek Books, an imprint of The Ohio State University Press, [2019] | Includes bibliographical references. | "Winner of the 2017 The Ohio State University Press/"The Journal" Charles B. Wheeler Poetry Prize"
Identifiers: LCCN 2018038782 | ISBN 9780814255162 (pbk. ; alk. paper) | ISBN 0814255167 (pbk. ; alk. paper)
Subjects: LCSH: American poetry—21st century.
Classification: LCC PS3614.E563 L48 2019 | DDC 811/.6—dc23
LC record available at https://lccn.loc.gov/2018038782

Cover design by Christian Fuenfhausen
Text design by Juliet Williams
Type set in Adobe Palatino

CONTENTS

||||||

||||||

CELL WATCH: STRIP CELL

Consider the cell not as you see it
but as it comes to be: a world
unto itself, the garden, uncharted
and rife with wildness, its beasts unnamed.
One man to one small room—you
grant him dominion so that he might
render the room expansive and rich,
his kingdom, stretch his mind
indefinitely. But since this is the beginning
of the world, it's up to you
to define the edges, contour
the known, to introduce the common
language: show him how this world
is nothing more than God's hand
grenade spinning through the air.
From the burning, you won't save him.
You'll build a room within a room,
another world to hold what's left
of this one. A box, rough pomegranate
wood, inlaid. Inside, a body's rough
material, a gift to God, a rib.

PASTORAL

Think of the work you will do
with your hands as the good,
good work, think of
the earth. If to tie a man
down in war is an act
of love, then think of the sows
your father raised, how
you called them in, held them
down, and how warm
and pink. And the meat goes to market
and a man goes to war
and here you must learn
to hang or be hanged.
If someone's throat in your hand
grows too warm, remember
to keep him talking, long after
he has said what you need
him to say, remember how you worked
the cow's ripe udder, long after
the calf was weaned. Glean something
useful: a name or a street
or the last day his father was seen.
And should he cry out
in the darkness, think of the way
you called out when your father
first bled a sow, think of
the voice in your throat calling
out, and your father's voice loud over yours
calling *hush*. Saying, *Mercy, this
is the way all things be.* And if the blood
on your hands grows too dark,
think of the bright pail of milk, its froth,
how you made something good

long after the calf had grown
      cold, how you made something good
with your hands, with your warmth,
      there in the warm and lonely dark.

FITNESS TEST

In the beginning there was a whole
lot of nothing, the darkness and the void
curling around God's ankles, loyal dogs,

God's silence tethering each to each.
We know what role a man's rib played,
that bone: more tooth than rib,
its hunger and desire

for a woman's body to sink itself
into. Think of the animals as made
of ribs or teeth, that God only invented
two kinds of figures, one bent

on consumption, one to be consumed.
In a small room, they'll hold you
up to the light, inspect then test
your bearings. If they're content that you

have yet to be eaten, that you have,
in fact, been eating others all along,
then they'll use someone like you.
They'll call you in. Then call the dogs.

TAPETUM LUCIDUM

I'm asked if I want to see
what it looks like and I say
yes before I know I'm saying
yes. This isn't news:
boys and a gun and a cat
left dead. This is upstate
New York and I'm thirteen
and a veterinarian shows me
how it works—how to shine
a light in the animal's eyes,
make them glow like two
green fruit. When I cut in
I expect shimmer, some
hidden iridescence, tissue
spun like thread. I want to see
what the cat must have seen—
the barrel raised, that crack
of sound, of dread—the eye
gives like a grape beneath
the blade. I bring it down.
The eye says what it can. And not
yet knowing what I'll know of men,
I shine a light inside to see
the dark recede, a hunted thing.

[THE BARS LASH LIGHT ACROSS HIS BODY, AND HE]

The bars lash light across his body, and he
contracts like a pupil, like a Black-Eyed
Susan's center, wind-stripped. The bars lash light across
his pupils, eyes unshining, unlike those of better animals
who stalk at night. The ones, somewhere, men lash to see
inside, pink organs flush with blood, bodies bathed
in sterile light. He grows thin, here, in the day's last light,
and the bars, unshining, absorb darkness like blood.
He lowers his black eyes, his organs purring,
better animals, still finding their way in the dark.
Somewhere, a body's lashed and bound by weather,
and the cross of a rifle's scope flits like an eyelash.
　　　The bars lash light across his back, and he
　　　becomes a stripped and weathered cross.

[LIKE A WIDENING PUPIL, THE DARK TOUCHES]

Like a widening pupil, the dark touches
everything, spreading its wound over
the lakes and fields you cannot see, over
dilapidated barns and rundown livestock,
where your father prepares a carcass. In your mind,
you see him lower the bled body, ready the water
for scalding. In the dark you'll ready the water,
though here it must be cold. You'll ready the cloth.
The wall between your charge and you is thin.
You hear him lean against it. The sum
of him no more than bone and gristle. It's late fall.
Your father will rig the carcass in the rafters,
> let the weather work its chill into the meat.
> He'll section the body. It will be cured.

[HE BECOMES A STRIPPED AND WEATHERED CROSS]

He becomes a stripped and weathered cross
and whittles away his body's rot: he softens
his rib cage's keel, his wrists burned sore
with rope. The worn night around him
heaves, swells, until he begins
to believe it's water that's filling his cell,
that his bare frame lifts to the rafters.
He imagines his body's a raft, deadwood
lashed together, cutting the dark toward
the animals and the ark on the shore. He
imagines he wrecks alongside them,
and though they cry and cry with their animal
       tongues, though their notes sound worn,
       he imagines they're calling him home.

[THE WALL BETWEEN YOUR CHARGE AND YOU IS THIN]

The wall between your charge and you is thin
as a membrane, porous as the skin that hangs
from your father's rafters, hardening in the cold.
Harden yourself against the man who will not
weather another season on your watch, against
the tools you use to make him speak. Boundless,
the winter field has forgotten what it knows
of rows and fences, turned earth. It stares
blankly through the window as your father
sections the carcass. You cut a board into pieces
the length of a man. Like a stretcher
or a box lid. You lean the boards against the wall
      and for once you feel nothing,
        your face a field in winter.

[HE IMAGINES THEY'RE CALLING HIM HOME]

He imagines they're calling him home
and his body's a home he must leave
to get there: he follows a path he's marked
with his nails and scalp, teeth that speak
his name. He leaves a rib to point
the way around a bend, an organ where
the road first forks. The animals come
down from the mountains, receive him
into their bellies. Inside them, he crosses
into the woods, becomes a better animal.
He begins to see the dark lift, sees you
in the distance weighed down
      by the weight of your own skin
      or the weight of carrying his.

[THE WINTER FIELD HAS FORGOTTEN WHAT IT KNOWS]

The winter field has forgotten what it knows
and so you do the work you know you must—
the meat chills slowly and hardens
on your father's watch and every inch
of it will have its use, and every inch of it
will fuel another's warmth—and so you must
believe the chill's enough to make a man
talk, to cure his conscience so that he gives
himself up, before you bind his arms to a board
again, before you bind his arms to his legs
again, a position that reminds you of tying
hogs, how it renders a man useless,
      every inch of him, so you pray
      the chill's enough to make a man—

[HE BEGINS TO SEE THE DARK LIFT, SEES YOU]

He begins to see the dark lift, sees you
lifting his body, his skin hanging
loose from rafters of bone, and he watches
through a window in his skull, his own
room, as you lift his body, which he
knows is made of water, which he knows
to be cold and everywhere, inside the animals
and under the fields, spreading its wound
over all you cannot see, although you carry
him now on your back like a cross,
like something too bright to look at,
as if he might, at any moment, burn
      the world down with his gaze,
      with the singular heat of God's face.

FAWN

Caught beneath a car but found alive,
the fawn screams but doesn't kick,
and it's too late. Her spine is crushed.
I try to hold her still. I didn't know
how bright her spots would be,
her dappled coat, my shaking hand
across her flank as if to wipe her clean.
Her eyes so wide, so close to mine,
I see my entire face inside.
It's years before a boy will throw me
to the ground, and years before I'll dream
his face, so close to mine, and scream
myself awake. I'm still a girl. I still believe
in wild things, that the startled animal
in my chest is not the fawn I carry in a bag,
wrapped and tied, like a gift, or grief.

AMERICAN ICON

Like a mother's throw
blanket over his shoulders,
like a little piece of home.
Like a homemade costume
any child wears, standing on
his mother's canned goods, striking
a pose and making a face, though
he can't see. He can't see. Witch
or monk or Jesus incarnate,
the wires are live. Like a real live
wire, he jumps. Like hopscotch
or rope. Like nothing a child
couldn't name. Hasn't seen.
Like nothing, like a game.

BARREL

As in what a child crouches behind
when he plays a hiding game. As in
what holds the grain, what waters
the horses. As in what a man stands on
when he's made to stand for hours,
what puts him on display. As in you look
it in the eye to see inside, and wait
to see who blinks.

ALL THE GAMES WE KNOW

Some kind of wild man, some
collar or noose to yoke this kind

of animal, wild, to a handler, so
that he crawls low, the collar

loose and then pulled taut
to tug him into place: he must be

taught. X marks the spot and he
must hit his mark, so we drag

our man, our skinny dog, dogs
at his heels. The dogs are barking

and our man doesn't want to
play, whimpers and pees.

What do we call this part
of the show, when the animals

all go wild like some kind of dance
but no one knows the moves?

We try all the games we know.
We say *don't move* or *move faster*

when what we want is to be
entertained. We shake

the photo until he fills
the frame.

CHAMBER

As in music, as in a division of the heart.
As in a grave, or a small room, or a house
for a doll or a bullet. As in the body is material
and a bullet shapes it. As in the long hall that stretches
between two people. As in singing, what shapes
the music as it comes barreling down.

PLAYING POSSUM

Saw a girl in half, boxed-in
      a cut box, the what-in-the
-world of her body still whole:
      the microphone wails
a high and lonely note.
      Refuses to transmit.
When they left him to hang
      they shackled his arms

behind him and when
      they returned the joke was still
funny: blood ran from his mouth
      like a faucet had turned on.
It's really that simple. His body
      leaks blood like a faucet, like
some old rusted spout, just a man
      playing possum with a bag
on his head. A man playing

a man now irreparably
      dead. Remember the girl
emerged whole, to our
      applause and delight. See her
laughing face bent over his, his
      body packed in ice. And
the joke is still. A photograph.
      A glove for scale.

WHERE WE ARE

What's come undone: the knots we practice
      in our sleep, on our own wrists. When a body
stops writhing, we imagine fish
      on the floor of a boat, heaving
until they don't. What Abraham couldn't have
      known: the quiet untying of a body
gone slack, the hands' work light and fast.
      God never said *here I am* and there's no one
here to ask. Where we are, the quiet pools
      like water. We wash our hands.
We put away the rope.

DEBRIDEMENT

In my childhood bedroom, my newborn
niece pressed to my shoulder, I walk
and pace to soothe her down to sleep.

I can't find the notebook
I could've sworn was here, stored
among old photographs and books.

I want to call down the narrow hall
of years that stretches back
to the summers I spent watching

the vet open each animal
like a lacquered jewel box
holding one breakable heirloom.

The breakable body I inherited
carries me still. Tonight, I bend my knees
to keep my niece asleep, press her animal

heat against my cheek. She grows heavy
and limp. As a girl, I said *by the skin
of my teeth* to mean *there but for the grace of*

the nurses who brought me back when
one lung collapsed. I want to call
into the bright room where

I later stood, looking over the vet's shoulder,
learning other ways a body breaks: *a dog can shake
its prey to snap its neck.* I want to say *by the skin*

of my teeth to mean the way I'll learn to carry
myself by the scruff of the neck, through all
the years ahead. Instead, I walk with my niece

and imagine the notebook I can't find, my girlhood
scrawl, what notes I left myself. How carefully
I wrote it down: the ways we close the skin

with thread. The ways a wound reopens.
And how, with what in mind, we look inside.

AT HOLMESBURG PRISON

All I saw before me were acres of skin. It was like a farmer
seeing a fertile field for the first time.
—DR. ALBERT KLIGMAN

If one takes the bird's eye
view, it's easy to see
how a field becomes
a fine-tuned system
designed to give us
exactly what we want:
row after row of finely
turned earth, pliant
beneath specific tools,
which we sharpen
in dark houses after
a long winter's sleep,
which we drag across
the earth until it yields
a pattern we can work
with, a matrix we bless
with growth, control
for weeds, eradicate
what shouldn't take.
We want to push
the boundaries without
giving way to disarray.
To see what might
survive these methods
is what we want, to raze
what fails us. Summon rain.
Under ideal conditions,
it's anybody's game.

PANOPTICON

Watch the sprawl of bodies before you, the tower an eye
you occupy, a gaze that burns their backs as they bend
before you, performing their tasks, labor that divides
and multiplies like the cells of a hive. Sweetness
too is found in work, sweat that releases sins, skin soft
with salt. See that they build a city that does not rise
but spreads like honey, like a rhizome, slowly, a controlled
and lateral home. Only this way can you watch the horizon,
its habits, the moon. How moving bodies become
one, like a lung, rising and falling
in unison.

AT EAST MISSISSIPPI CORRECTIONAL

Around the eye of a storm, matter's
rearranged beyond recognition, beyond
repair. As if through an old, scratched lens,
the old minutiae carry on beneath
the frozen lake, while out of sight
and behind bars men deemed beyond
repair work their daily recognitions:
they toil and repeat their movements,
until they replicate an old domestic rite,
how wild dogs came down the mountains
to sleep beside us, how over time
we let them. Inside a cell, a man
weaves hair to make a leash.
Catches a wild rat and calls it *dog*,
sells it to the highest bidder.
Over time, the rat's teeth grow
and curl until they pierce its gums
like the eyelid of a lake. Drops of blood
like fish begin to surface. Inside a cell,
a man beyond recognition replicates
an old domestic rite, something tender,
and out of the corner of your eye you see
him caught in the eye of a storm, where
everything seems to slow like a careful
kind of work, the kind that repeats itself,
the hand's insistent gesture to rend
the animal free from its own teeth.

EUPHEMISM

It wasn't my dog. It wasn't
my father holding the animal
and kneeling beside her. It
didn't happen while I was
in another city, looped
on sedatives and pain meds,
waiting by the phone for
my father's voice, in another
city, to tell me it was done.
That was years away. The dog
was old and not my dog,
and a man who was not my father
knelt beside her, and I knelt
beside him. And I stayed
very still while the dog's legs
splayed and she slumped
to the floor. And I went
very quietly for the mop
while a man sat with his dog,
while the vet left him alone
in the room. I wanted to do
a good job. To do as I was told.
I waited and a man knelt with his back
to the door, to me. Heard him say,
God damn you. God damn, and mistook
his grief for something sharp and mean.
And then, over his shoulder, *you can stay.*
Into the room, into the air, *please stay.*

PRISONER'S CINEMA WITH SAINTS CATHERINE AND LUCY

Lit by a million specks of light,
    all your dust turns holy.
What's rotten in you burns

    and burns. You, a shadow-
you, gone glowing
    Catherine wheel, a spoked

gloaming. You know lead can lodge
    into an animal's skull, turn
the skull into a lit temple

    of its wanderings, and this is how
you understand the fabled bowl
    a saint carries, its hollow lit

by the eyes it cradles and the saint
    eyeless and God-filled. You are not
eyeless and God is nowhere

    to witness how you become
the wheel and the body it breaks,
    a spectacle of light you cannot fathom

until you fathom it—flooded
    as you are with shadow, darkness
taut as an animal's shank

until it ripples at your touch. Pools
    in the bowl your hands make.
Then breaks.

PARABLES

1. The light of the body is the eye

And the lights are eyes
        that watch us. And the lights
are ears to hear us pour forth
        the dark in us. If you don't have
any darkness, the lights will make
        a shadow and you can claim it.
Once, your mother carried
        a lamp to your bedside
to keep the dark at bay
        and you slept. And you slept
the sleep that pins a body
        down, that leaves a body limp.
The lamps are eyes, fixed wide. And now
        we see ourselves as we are seen.
And now our shadows draw
        quickly from our feet, rear up
like beasts. They pin us down.

2. *And it fell: and great was the fall*

You have given us a house
        built on the sand. And you
have given us a house built
        for the dead. And all around

the sand grates skin as salt
        corrodes a structure over time.
Over time, we rust. Patina spreads

its name across the floor, and you
        check our eyes for signs
of what's to come, for birds

on the horizon, for missing ships.
        With sand we fill and refill bags
to stabilize the walls against

the flood, against the dead
        we will become, who keen
and keen like stormwinds
        at our door.

3. *And the waters prevailed*

When the flood comes, we understand it first
with our mouths because we fill like heavy vases, our tongues
wilted flowers. We are told the flood is God because we are filled,
because we are heavy with His love: God's truth inside
waiting and waiting while they flush our nostrils with water,
so that it might be delivered to them like an animal stumbling,
legs shaky and bent, eyes squinting in the new light: squinting to see us
there on the shore at the end of one weak plank, calling and calling.
They speak of the truth as a near-drowned thing. Tell how Noah
saved two of each beast. How after forty days
the sun wore a kind face, even as it fell
into the sea.

4. *That they may not understand*

If the tower of our voice rises in song, if it reaches
God. If the tower is high and strong and sends
up names, if our names reach heaven, then from
the speakers they send forth a plague of music to drown
us out. Then from God's name resounding within the walls
does brick tumble down to dust. To dust they return us,
splintered and chipped so that God cannot receive us,
our cries garbled, rubble in our mouths. They pull
forth our tongues, wag them around until we call
out in the language we are destined to praise:
until the city we love is forgotten.
So the city we love is erased.

5. *And the graves were opened*

      And the walls that they erected
fell around us. And the walls
      within those walls fell around us.
So the wood spit out its nails
      and we saw their rusted heads.
Saw each box spit out
      a body, each body pierced
by thorns. The sky warped
      and split, as if by force.
We lifted each other, lifted dust.
      The tombs yawned wide as days.
We girthed the graves. We blinked
      our eyes and the Earth was still
the Earth.

PRISONER'S CINEMA WITH NEWS FROM HOME

no one among us has seen God but this
morning a lamb was born and shook itself its cry
into the world and I thought of the Earth
spinning and the godless movement of men
toward each other in darkness our cells
spinning in our blood and the walls
of cells we touch one another without seeing
distance between us and I thought of the lamb
among us the morning cries into the world
between us spinning I thought of the distance
we touch without seeing one another
among us God moves no one only this

AT OREGON STATE PENITENTIARY

In 1973, Dr. Carl Heller irradiated 67 inmates' testes as part of his research for the Atomic Energy Commission.

A bomb grows on a tree,
in time. And we will bless you
not with water but with fire,
will burn the name of our Lord
into your flesh so that you move
closer to his glory, his heat,
though you will know him
soon in the kiss of earth,
the fallow earth beneath
your feet, as it was before
God, before Eve. And
because we cannot save
your children from the sins
you will not confess,
because we know you
to be wicked, sick, we offer
you up to the Lord as men
in whom fire will thrive,
spread, divide, as men
in whom blessed half-lives
glow divine. In you
a singular universe expands
over time. And from you
we glean what we need:
God's seed, sickened, the end
of your family line. The atomic
sun still shines and the world
spins closer to disaster. God's
heat. For us, you become
scorched earth. In time,
you turn obsolete.

PRAYER FOR MERCY

—and who among us
          has not begged for Mercy
and bent his head
          in prayer, that Mercy
bends our necks
          upon the block—
and bless *the pretty maid*s
          all in a row, that they may
move cleanly in their duty,
          let fall their gleaming teeth
with the precision of a clock—
          and Mercy from our mouths
hear you our prayer that runs
          down our chins sure as wine
turns to blood—and to you
          we trust our headless bodies
to be counted and weighed—
          from *silver bells and cockle
shells* we bleat your name,
          shill Mercy, mother,
Mercy, your name—

AT FOLSOM WOMEN'S FACILITY

Between 2005 and 2013, multiple women held at Folsom and other
California prisons were sterilized without their consent.

The warden comes down
like Gabriel with news
of the Lord that you are
blessed among women
and opens the door to the cell
you keep, the blessed door
of the tomb you keep, unearths
you with news and leads you,
among women, to a room
where God waits in blue
gloves with men who
lower their instruments
in the light of the Lord,
the city of the Lord within
you, blessed among cities,
an instrument of God.
And God's men have come
to fell the soft scaffolding,
so that you, who *know not*
a man, may know only
your body as God's
empty room, an empty
tomb you keep, so that
the warden should come
to your door like Gabriel
with news of the world, the war,
with the blinding light
of the Lord just out of reach.

PROCEDURE

Leukemia vaccination on the left. Rabies
on the right. I begin to see the animals
in terms of where afflictions might appear:
ear mites and hookworms, mange or fleas or ticks,
deadly Parvo that can kill a dog in days.
At night, I sleep in the daughter's old room,
beneath a paper cutout on the ceiling,
a teenage outline filled in with glossy parts
from magazines—the mouth is many mouths,
the arms are made of arms. When the legs
of one sick dog give out and there's nothing
left to do, I focus on the steps we take,
prepare. As if this kind of repetition
is a form of prayer that could save
a body from itself. But since it can't,
I take the outline of the animal
on the wall, a map of what's inside,
the body's glossy red. I cut the bad parts out
and rearrange them into something else:
I shape the legs into a giant mouth. I sit
and wait to hear what it will say.

AT PITCHESS DETENTION CENTER

The Active Denial System uses electromagnetic radiation to stun targets with heat. In 2010, Pitchess Detention Center sought to install it.

It's no different than the game
      we played as children: a dry leaf,
a magnifying glass to focus
      the sun's ray, a little smoke
for show, to show the others
      how the thing gets done. The leaf
never amounts to the fire
      you would hope, but master
the basics and what you flame next
      depends on what's at hand: a twig
or two, a piece of paper, a line of ants.
      From a distance, you'll need
a steady grip, a real keen eye,
      great aim. Once they feel
the heat, it's only a matter
      of time until they flee. How
a thing gets done: you set them
      running right into God's arms,
and then you set them free.

CONFINEMENT PRAYER

Consider what you cannot
see and how you must
proceed: if the wind presses
itself to your chest, you must
make room for it within you,
you must make of your chest
a house for wind. Consider
what you cannot carry:
make of your body a room
where the dead come to rest.
In this room where names rise
as air, you must leave your bones
clean and cold. Like a field
where nothing takes. Where no
one comes to carry you home.

Lethal injection typically depends on a three-drug cocktail: a sedative or anesthetic, a paralyzing agent, and a drug that stops the heart.

Execution absent an adequate sedative thus produces a nightmarish death: The condemned prisoner is conscious but entirely paralyzed, unable to move or scream his agony, as he suffers "what may well be the chemical equivalent of being burned at the stake."

—JUSTICE SONIA SOTOMAYOR, DISSENTING *ARTHUR V. DUNN,* 2017

Patients should never confuse the death chamber with the operating room, lethal doses of execution drugs with anesthetic drugs, or the executioner with the anesthesiologist.

—J. JEFFREY ANDREWS, MD, 2014 SECRETARY OF THE AMERICAN BOARD OF ANESTHESIOLOGY

LETHAL THEATER

If I tell you my body is a mausoleum
and a needle houses ghosts, then you
should know I know them all
by name: that Ether is Letheon
is Lethe is forgetfulness is how
I remember the bend in the river
where my blood turns sharply,
where the ghosts of condemned
men cannot cross. Is where the needle
points the way home, across the river,
though the men cannot cross, though I
return every time. If I tell you there are hands
that bring me back, then you should know
there are hands that hold men down.
If I tell you that men are always drowning
in me, that the bend in the river is the place
I first wake into the world: this is how
a man dies. This is how we kill him.

||||||

PROTOCOL A:

If gas, it's kind to tell them to *breathe deeply*. If you administer
the drugs by injection, it's kind to get the vein on the first try.
Sometimes they'll arch their backs and call out *this isn't working,*
sometimes they'll help you find the right vein. It's best
if it works the first time. In the surgical theater, draw
back the curtain so one can see the scene as it's been staged.
Drape a sheet over the body before you begin.

||||||

I open and close my fist and wait for one blue root
to emerge under my skin, hold still every time. I am
the model of an ideal patient, a doll on which to practice.
The nurse's eyes are two dark bulbs in mine
and she plants the needle. By the wrist, I'm led
to water. It's not gentle, but it's not unkind.
This isn't where I die. I wait in my brain's thicket,
and a sedative disrupts the nerves. They reach
their branches. A smokescreen so that the men
may approach. Soon, burning. The kind
of smoke one sees for miles, if one sees at all.
I wait for their faces. I wait by their graves.

||||||

WITNESS:

There's sort of a ritual, I guess, to these inmates pounding on the glass.
They're pounding on the glass and making a bit of a scene.
And we're waiting to go inside the building, and people are talking
about their cats, and their remodels, and the radio's on.

||||||

PROTOCOL B:

You must secure the bodies equally,
        all men equal in death. If gas, it's kind
to tell them to *breathe deeply.* If you administer
        a lethal injection, it's kind
to get the line on the first try. Sometimes
        they'll arch their backs and call out
this isn't working, sometimes they'll help you
        find the right vein, sometimes it works
the first time. Pause and bow your head
        according to the preordained script.
Bow your head. Hope it's quick.

||||||

WITNESS:

About two years ago I had to euthanize my dog.
And you don't want to do that.
But it's the most humane way to do it.
Having not seen the others, I think it's the most humane.
I had never seen anybody die.
It's the only time I've seen anybody die.

||||||

In a burning city, no one comes back
for the dead, but I keep coming back
to the bend in the river, where the smoke
swallows you whole, Claude, and it swallows
me whole so that I can be healed, halved,
split, threaded, a needle-eyed slit that opens
into poppy or violet landscape, where one
violent color becomes another before
I can tell the surgeons to find you, though no
one is ever looking, not here, where they open
me into the brightest evening purple
you've ever seen, while you're drowning
in the smoke, the needle's wildfire
in our veins, and I try to tell them how
it hurts, where our bodies open
and close against the needle and knife,
how you open and close your fist against
a needle's precise pinch, while I close beneath
another needle's stitch, how hot the blood,
the breath, the bone, how quickly winter comes,
collapsed vein or flooded lung, how blue
the light, Claude, how precisely cold
a river runs, how precisely cold and blue
your body turns in this light, arms outstretched
or raised, how fast it comes, when where
we are is where the living leave,
is where I always leave alive,
please tell me, Claude, what do we see?

||||||

WITNESS:

There was disagreement among the nine of us about what we saw.
We were talking about what happened, what happened, what happened,
    what did you see?

IIIIII

PROTOCOL B:

Call the task at hand *get the man dead.*
      Take turns playing dead-man-walking.
Clock it so that death comes right
      on time. Flank the surrogate prisoner.
Surrogate can fight or cry or collapse or kick
      against the restraints. To get the man dead,
open and close the curtains, the chamber's door,
      lower the gas canister, or insert the needle.
Say how long he sits or stands. When it's all done,
      when no one moves, say *stop.*

||||||

PROTOCOL A:

      Patients sometimes wake up and call out
on the way to recovery: they want water, a mother.
      Push the gurney, lift your voices over theirs, say
the procedure went well. Lift their bodies or secure them in place,
      in case the drugs don't take. Draw the curtain in case.

||||||

When the vein won't show
its blue, I imagine the needle
is a divining rod that points
the way to water, and this is where
I keep you, Claude, just beyond
the mound of earth where the needle
lands short of the river, where
my skin swells and never gives
you away. It's useless to fill
a pocket of skin, a small delay,
and it can burn like hell, and this
too, you know, though I try to
keep you from the nurses, though
the nurses find you anyway. They
try and try until the needle's in. Until
the river floods its banks
and carries you away, and where I go
isn't as cold, and they always say
I go for my own good.

||||||

PROTOCOL B:

Sometimes a man wakes up. Sometimes a man can stay alive,
    or the drugs burn like fire. A needle can come loose.
It can take time. A man could lift his head. Could say,
    it's come undone. Could come undone.

||||||

WITNESS:

I would do it again.
How would you not want to do that?

||||||

I've begun to see you in the flowers I learn
to name the summer after one lung collapses
in recovery, and I fall in love with all the gods
and myths. I'm only ten. I hear purple loosestrife
lustrife and think it's beautiful, and fall in love
with weeds. I don't yet know that Morpheus
the god of dreams belongs to us, that the drug
to which he lends his name runs through
my childhood, all through my blood, takes root.
I don't yet know you'll shoot up with the same,
that your veins will be so hard to find
you'll almost cheat the executioner. At ten,
I outlive death and learn the names
of other things that refuse to die: I cut
loosestrife at the root then wish it back.
I dream a plot of dirt is not a grave but grace,
and purple loosestrife brings you back
and says your name.

||||||

WITNESS:

This probably speaks to the way we do things in this country,
but I'm trying to remember what his victim's name was—

|||||||

PROTOCOL B:

If your wife wants to know if it wears on you,
        tell her the answer's in your work, in your devotion
to the team, even if some of you see men's faces
        in the faces of strangers in the supermarket
or at your son's baseball games, beneath the rim
        of someone else's cap. Shoulder it well
enough: the weight of this particular labor
        should carry over into tenderness, the steadiness
with which you lift your sleeping child. The child
        who, after nightmares, settles in your bed,
goes limp and heavy in your arms
        when you carry him back down the hall.
Sleep the sleep of the dead. In the morning,
        kiss your wife, then do it again.

IIIIII

WITNESS:

This particular night there was a playoff baseball game on.
The Yankees were playing.
There was one reporter—you probably don't care about this—
but it's one of those things in all my years of reporting that just sticks with me—
she brought a date. She was dating a cop at the time.
She said she needed moral support.
He was able to get into the prison I guess, because he was a cop.
But they just sat there and cuddled and held hands all night.
It was distasteful.
But, you know, we listened to a baseball game for most of the night.

||||||

I want to ask you where you went, and if there's water.
I want to know if grief ebbs in death, or if you still
press it to your chest like a lover, doll, or daughter.

‖‖‖‖‖

A sweet smell like anesthesia
strange tree blooming
and I ask a woman, *where does that smell come from*
Claude, she can't answer me
strange tree sweet flower
blooming in my brain's thicket I fall
to my knees in loosestrife
I lose you here I'm held
down all spring all sweetness
by the mask they held to my mouth

||||||

WITNESS:

There are images that come up sometimes at odd times.
The smell of bleach will do it to me.

|||||||

Dear You, whose face I see as if underwater and at a distance,
at the bottom of a lake I dive although you are always
beyond reach and I am scared to open my eyes underwater,
to look at what's been done to you, what we do
to each other: I say your name when I wake,
your name recorded in the prison book
before you go under, before you seize and thrash
against the drugs, and your name is the burnt
air on my tongue, the sweet air I breathe everywhere
I go, the smell of which brings me to my knees,
air heavy with spring and manufactured
sleep, a gas that lulls me under, or your veins
run full with numbness that leaves you
slumped and empty, or my veins run full
with the same, until I'm pulled awake by the taste
of your name in my mouth, my burnt tongue
in my mouth, until I pull the mask from my face,
the needle from my vein, turn toward you
and say, Dear You, Dear Wronged and Forgotten,
everywhere I look, I am looking for you—

||||||

NOTES

"American Icon" is based on a photograph first thought to be of Ali Shalal Qaissi, a professor of theology who survived torture at Abu Ghraib, and then of another prisoner, Abdou Hussain Saad Faleh, called "Gilligan" by US soldiers. Sometimes referred to as "The Hooded Man," the image shows a man on a box with a hood over his head with electrical wires attached to his fingers.

"All the Games We Know" is loosely based on a photograph of Lynndie England dragging a man by a leash at Abu Ghraib.

"Playing Possum" borrows text from soldiers' testimony during the wrongful death investigation of Manadel al-Jamadi, a prisoner who died from torture while in US custody at Abu Ghraib. The poem also refers to a photograph of US Army Specialist Sabrina Harman giving a thumbs-up sign while posing next to Al-Jamadi's corpse.

"At Holmesburg Prison": Dr. Albert Kligman oversaw dangerous and unethical dermatological tests on inmates at Holmesburg, from approximately 1951 to 1974. Kligman also oversaw government-backed LSD and dioxin tests at the same facility, the results of which led to lifelong physical and mental trauma for many of his test subjects.

"At East Mississippi Correctional" is based on an ACLU report about the facility, filed in 2013, which found that "rats often climb over prisoners' beds, and some prisoners capture the rats, put them on makeshift leashes, and sell them as pets to other inmates."

"Prisoner's Cinema with Saints Catherine and Lucy" and "Prisoner's Cinema with News from Home": The term *prisoner's cinema* refers to the hallucinations brought about by long-term isolation or confinement in the dark.

"At Oregon State Penitentiary": Dr. Carl Heller's tests extended beyond Oregon; several Washington prisons were also involved in his studies. Men who were subjected to testicular irradiation were often sterilized at the conclusion of the trials. Of those who were not, at least four of them fathered children with severe birth defects. Because no follow-up studies were conducted, the exact numbers are likely much higher.

"Prayer for Mercy": The italicized sections are taken from an old nursery rhyme, "Mary, Mary, Quite Contrary." Some theories posit that *pretty maids* refers to guillotines, while *silver bells and cockle shells* may be names of torture instruments.

"At Folsom Women's Facility" borrows text from Luke 1:26–38, KJV. Approximately thirty-nine women at Folsom and three other California prisons were sterilized without consent between 2005 and 2013.

"At Pitchess Detention Center": The Active Denial System was developed by Raytheon for use in Afghanistan in 2010 but was ultimately withdrawn due to concerns it could be used for torture. Instead, the instrument underwent a six-month trial at Pitchess Detention Center in California.

"Lethal Theater" references the botched execution of Claude Jones. All witness sections are compiled from interviews conducted with two AP journalists who witnessed separate executions in Utah. The title of the poem, and book, is a nod to Dwight Conquergood's article, "Lethal Theatre: Performance, Punishment, and the Death Penalty" (*Theatre Journal* 54.3 [2002]: 339–67).

ACKNOWLEDGMENTS

I'd like to extend my utmost gratitude to the editors and staff at the following publications, where several of these poems first appeared, sometimes in earlier versions or under different titles:

Crazyhorse: "At Holmesburg Prison," "Parables (flood)," "Prisoner's Cinema with News from Home," and "War Pastoral"
Guernica: "Prisoner's Cinema with Saints Catherine and Lucy"
The Los Angeles Review of Books Quarterly: "At Pitchess Detention Center" and "Cell Watch: Strip Cell"
The Los Angeles Review: "At Folsom Women's Facility," "Chamber," and "Where We Are"
The National Poetry Review: "Panopticon"
Pleiades: "Confinement Prayer" and "Playing Possum"
Public Pool: "Tapetum Lucidum"
Southern Indiana Review: "Fawn"
32 Poems: "Parables (lamp)" and "Parables (flood)"

Re-publications:

Verse Daily: "Prisoners' Parable of the Lamp"
Poetry Daily: "At Holmesburg"
Motionpoems: "Cell Watch: Strip Cell" directed by Jane Morledge

For her faith in my work and for selecting this manuscript for publication, I'm hugely indebted to Kathy Fagan. Enormous thanks to all the readers for the Wheeler Prize, the incredible staff at *The Journal* and The Ohio State University Press, and to Editor-in-Chief Kristen Elias Rowley for shepherding these poems into a book.

I'm beyond grateful to the University of Utah Department of English for their support, and for a Clarence Snow Fellowship, which gave me focused time and resources to work on these poems. To my teachers and mentors, Molly Bendall, Katharine Coles, Jay Jacobson, Paisley Rekdal, Angela Smith, Jacqueline Osherow, and Barry Weller: thank you for pushing me to read and write widely and wildly. I'm lucky to have you in my corner.

Heartfelt thanks to the good folks at the Civitella Ranieri Foundation, and those in residence with me there when this book began in earnest; and to Persea Books and Gabriel Fried for the gift of that time. To the smart, kind, and thoughtful readers at the Sewanee Writers' Conference, and to Maurice Manning and Mark Jarman's workshop: thank you for your keen feedback and for essential discussions about violence and the stage. Thank you to Douglas Kearney, who saw early poems in this book and told me to keep going.

Thank you to the two Associated Press journalists, J. D. and R. G., for sharing your experiences and trusting me with your words. Thank you to all my students, especially those at the Utah State Prison, for never letting me forget how deeply language matters.

To Nora Ericson, Debbie Hummel, Julia Lyon, Natasha Mileusnic, and Sabrina Hiteshew Wilson, the incredible women in my Salt Lake writing group, thank you for your insightful feedback, for getting me out of the house, and for all the encouragement.

To those who lift me up, whose light and love and friendship make all things possible, and who read, edited, and otherwise helped me fashion and refashion this book, I offer my unending thanks: Jessica Rae Bergamino, Laura Bylenok, Catie Crabtree, Meg Day, Alex Distler, Chris Kondrich, and Joe Sacksteder. Special thanks to J. P. Grasser for the early morning prompts, sharp line edits, and unbridled enthusiasm despite my own reservations; to Claire Wahmanholm for reading carefully, for thoughts on order, and for sorting out my pronouns; to Tessa Fontaine, Sara Eliza Johnson, and Cori Winrock for making me face that last poem; and to Molly McCully Brown for being my grounding wire and for always keeping me company.

Thank you to my parents, Jack and Nancy, to whom I owe everything; to Vince, Laura, Lucia, and Violet; and to Larry, Mary, Danny, Shaun, and Helen. And finally, thank you to David, for your kind and generous heart, your love, and for this extraordinary life we share.

The Journal Charles B. Wheeler Poetry Prize

Lethal Theater
SUSANNAH NEVISON

Radioapocrypha
BK FISCHER

June in Eden
ROSALIE MOFFETT

Somewhere in Space
TALVIKKI ANSEL

The River Won't Hold You
KARIN GOTTSHALL

Antidote
COREY VAN LANDINGHAM

Fair Copy
REBECCA HAZELTON

Blood Prism
EDWARD HAWORTH HOEPPNER

Men as Trees Walking
KEVIN HONOLD

American Husband
KARY WAYSON

Shadeland
ANDREW GRACE

Empire Burlesque
MARK SVENVOLD

Innocence
JEAN NORDHAUS

Autumn Road
BRIAN SWANN

Spot in the Dark
BETH GYLYS

Writing Letters for the Blind
GARY FINCKE

Mechanical Cluster
PATTY SEYBURN

Magical Thinking
JOSEPH DUEMER